Pampù and the Plants

Laura Ebrahimi

ISBN:-10:149492014X
ISBN-13:978-1494920142

Dedicated to my mother

Since when I was little I was fascinated by her passion and knowledge about science.

I loved listening to her childhood stories, of her happy days spent in the country with her aunt in Tuscany near the coast and with another aunt in northern Italy by the mountains, mostly out in the fields with plants and animals.

I grew up thinking that my mom was a living encyclopedia. With her biology* degree, at a time when only a handful of women would get one, and most of all being in contact with nature much of her life, it came natural to her having me look and appreciate the beauty of the physical universe, directing my attention to those small details that people generally pass by without even noticing, like getting a close view at the veins in a leaf.

She would appreciate beauty 360 degrees, from the aesthetics of how something looks to the mechanics of how something works, to how it acts like a link in the chain of life. She was able to communicate it so well and so easy to follow that when I had to study science in school I hated it in complex textbooks.

Absorbing science casually through my mother got me curious about other fields too. I wanted to learn different languages and explore more regions of the world, probably to experience what is beyond the physical world, other cultures and the mechanics of the mind. But the love for plants has always followed me, adding beauty and interest to life.

My mom passed that love to me. I pass it to you through these tales. A pinch of botany* fuels the skeleton of each story, the creative vein dresses it up with words and imagination.

Laura Ebrahimi, aka Giala

CONTENTS

Introduction

Pampù is a special lady. She loves plants.

The plants view her and the whole human race as aliens.

Pampù and the plants always share some adventures together with peculiar interactions.

When Pampù is up to something with them, the plants respond and talk about it.

Though Pampù and the plants speak different languages and have different needs, they seem to have a common goal: survive and be happy together.

1 Pampù and the Begonia

Pampù went to the supermarket and bought a pot with some small, bright pink begonia plants. She put them in plain sight on a table by the living room window. She looks at them every day and when the soil is no longer moist she waters it. After about a month she realizes that the plants are no longer straight. They are bending towards the window where the natural light comes in.

Dialogue between the plants:

"We may have not noticed anything the first few days here, but now we are clearly bent towards the light!"

"The light must be very powerful, if we are attracted towards it even without our will."

"Today the alien has turned our pot 180 degrees. I feel dizzy and I lost my balance. Do you feel the same way?"

"Yes, I do. Pampù must have not been too happy to see us bent, so she may have rotated our pot hoping we would get straight again."

"But for how long can we stay up this time? After we resume a vertical position we might start bending once more."

"Then what should Pampù do to keep us upright?"

"She should move our pot to a spot where the light comes from all sides, just like how it is outside, under the sky, where we come from."

Pampù looks at them, almost as if she knew she was part of their conversation. Then she goes to her computer and after half an hour searching about begonias she moves the pot to a different room in the house, all surrounded by windows and under a skylight. Mission accomplished! In a few days her begonias get to be up and to stay straight. They are very happy to be finally settled.

2 Pampù and the Basil

Pampù goes to the supermarket and buys a packet of basil seeds. It is late spring, the perfect season to plant basil in a pot. Pampù puts the basil on the window sill in her bedroom.

Dialogue between the basil seeds:

"We do not understand why Pampù has put us in the bedroom rather than in the kitchen. Aliens generally use us to add flavor to their food."

After about two months the seeds have become seedlings, time to find out why they are in the bedroom!

"Do you notice that insects stay away from us? Those insects must hate scents, because we are very fragrant. No wonder Pampù keeps us here! We are a defense against annoying insects. We really are useful to the aliens, not just in the kitchen but also to ward off mosquitoes!"

3 Pampù and the Lettuce

Pampù has planted some lettuce in her backyard. The leaves will be good for her salads.

"I feel smaller. Pampù has harvested our leaves, our aerial part."

"I know but our central bud will make more leaves."

"What will happen then?"

"Same thing, our aerial part will be cut and it will grow back on from the base."

"Aliens say that fate shared is a joy! The important part of us, the root, has remained intact, so we will not die and we will continue to develop new leaves all through spring and summer until fall, when it gets too cold for us. We can find joy being together till the end of our annual cycle."

Pampù loves to have her fresh lettuce leaves with sour cream and strawberries.

4 Pampù and the Mushrooms

It is September, it has rained and it is hot. Pampù lives near a forest with chestnut trees. She did not sleep much last night due to the heat. She wakes up early morning and she decides to go into the woods to cool off in the shade and look for mushrooms. She leaves the house armed with a long, wooden stick to help clear her way through the bushes, to scout the ground for mushrooms and to scare snakes. Her beloved, faithful dog, Shirin, follows her like a shadow. The air is thick with the smell of musk, of fallen chestnut leaves and of porcini mushrooms. Pampù gently moves the chestnut leaves in the ground with her stick, hoping to find some hidden mushrooms but she is not having much luck. In one hour she has found only three large porcini and five ovoli. A strange wind starts blowing at irregular intervals, bringing to her nostrils the strong, pleasant scent of mushrooms and humus. Then she enters an area with a wind tunnel that instead has no smell.

Dialogue between the mushrooms

"Pampù didn't see me."

"She didn't see me either."

"She did not see us and she did not smell our carpet of mushrooms with at least 30 types of various sizes."

"How lucky we are, we were all in danger of being picked, especially the many of us with a large cap. Aliens love to fry the big porcini caps and to pickle the small mushrooms in jars with oil and vinegar. Only the very tiny ones just developing from the mycelium, our growing base, would have been spared."

"Those babies would have not like to be alone, without the company of the big grown up!"

Pampù is getting tired after a few hours walk in the forest and her dog looks thirsty. She goes back home and she cooks her fresh mushrooms for lunch.

5 Pampù and the Asparagus

It is March and Pampù walks up a hill in search for wild asparagus. After she collects a bunch, she returns home and she puts them on the kitchen countertop next to a bundle of cultivated asparagus that her daughter had got at the supermarket. The two kinds of asparagus, so different in their appearance, look at each other and start talking.

Wild asparagus: "You, my friend, cultivated asparagus, do not brag about yourself, you may look more majestic than me, but my life is better than yours."

Cultivated asparagus: "How is that so?"

Wild asparagus: "I was born in freedom, camouflaged in the midst of green grass and protected by borders. I was picked from the ground only because this alien was able to spot me, otherwise I could have continued my life cycle and become adult like my brothers in the wild."

Cultivated asparagus: "Instead our life is short. We are all grown to be harvested and become food for the aliens because we taste good and we are loaded with nutrients."

Wild asparagus: "If the aliens find us we become food for them too but we are more flavorful because we are born spontaneously."

Cultivated asparagus: "Well, even if we live in different environments, we belong to the same family. I am happy Pampù has given us the opportunity to meet and share our existence."

Pampù cooks the asparagus in two different pots, using the same recipe, to test which one is better.

6 Pampù and the Capers

Pampù goes on vacation to sunny Italy. While she is walking along a path through an ancient field she sees a wall where in between the rocks there is a bit of space. To her surprise, she spots a plant she has never seen before, a caper bush in full bloom growing out of those tiny openings.

Dialogue between the capers:

"We live so well in this type of rocky environment under the sun! On a clear day we are exposed to the sun from morning to night and in this climate we produce many beautiful, delicate flowers."

"Well, we are humble plants, not showy, but at the same time we are very important because the aliens extract a substance from our flower buds that is good against allergies."

"Aliens use us also to add more flavor to their dishes."

"But when they get our buds, we won't get to have flowers."

"We are lucky we are not everywhere and we are not easy to find. This alien here seems to be a harmless tourist. She is just staring at us, almost as if she had never seen a caper bush before!"

Pampù now knows what a caper plant looks like. She had only seen capers in jars at the supermarket.

7 Pampù and the Potatoes

After the last spring frost, Pampù goes to the supermarket and buys a bag of potatoes. She needs some for cooking and some for planting, so she stores half the bag on a dark, cool, dry, shelf inside the pantry, and she puts the other half on the countertop by the window where in one or two days under the sunlight they will develop tiny green buds, the eyes, that she needs for planting. Then she digs a shallow hole in the ground with a shovel and she places each potato piece with an eye about a foot apart.

Dialogue between the potatoes:

"What's happening to us?"

"Pampù has divided us into several parts."

"What do we have in common now?"

"Well, each of us has at least one eye."

"What is the eye for?"

"From each eye we will grow a new potato."

"Why can't we see each other?"

"Don't worry, Pampù has put us in the ground, eye up, but we won't be in the dark for long, the light will help us develop a new plant from each eye, thanks to the reserve of nutrients we have in each piece."

After a few weeks …

"Hey, we can be happy again, before we were locked in a bag, now we are green plants, there is a lot of light and we can see each other again!"

Pampù has been patiently waiting for about two months, finally when the flowers appear she can harvest some young potatoes, being very careful not to pull the stems so the other potatoes can keep growing. When the leaves turn yellow, her full grown potatoes will be ready to go to her kitchen.

8 Pampù and the Bean Seeds

Pampù wants to plant beans in her garden after the last spring frost. She gets a bag of dried beans, she chooses a sunny spot, she prepares a small hole in the ground, she distributes the beans at a regular distance from each other and she covers them with soil.

Dialogue between the bean seeds:

"Before we could see the light, now we are in the dark."

"I feel some moisture that makes me swell."

"I do not know if it happens to you too, but I feel like I am moving even if no one touches me."

"My skin is no longer intact, something is growing downward, the root, and something is growing upward, the stem."

"It is happening to me as well and from what I hear to all of us here."

"Our body was dried before, now it is different and we can see the sun again."

"In just a few days two strange swollen leaves, the pods, have developed from our stems and now they are empty."

"Those pods were our food until our roots have become fully functional and we have grown new leaves that appear to be normal. The beauty is that we have changed color, we were white seeds and now we have become green seedlings."

"Could it be the light to make us change color?"

"Could it be that the seeds of all plants behave like this?"

"I think so and I'm happy."

"Yes, now we can see each other again and we are still together."

Pampù is looking at her beautiful bean crop and is happy too.

9 Pampù and the Beans

"We are dormant dried beans of various colors and sizes. We are all well stored together with our brothers without doing anything."

One day Pampù goes to school to do an experiment. She lines the inside of a glass container with a white absorbent paper towel and she positions some beans randomly between the glass and the paper. Then she puts soil inside the container and she waters it thoroughly.

"We do not understand the meaning of this adventure, we feel immersed in a humid environment. Pampù says that we are germinating."

"We start swelling and after two long days our seed coat breaks open. Pampù says that we are sprouting."

"Each of us starts growing some white threads downwards, the roots, then a stem upwards and finally small leaves. In this new life we lose connection with our old brothers, the dried beans that did not get to be in this adventure. We can only see the few of us lined up in the same position, like soldiers. We have become live plants. Pampù says that we are now in an active phase."

"We will make flowers and then we will become parents of bean pods. Aliens will harvest us fresh to go straight in their mouth, or they will let us dry on the plant under the sun, till we are dormant dried beans again."

Pampù tells her audience that beans were cultivated in Mexico and in Africa 7,000 years ago, and that later on Christopher Columbus sailed them from Cuba to introduce them to the European royal chefs.

°Pampù did not say that we come in 14,000 different types and that only 26 are good to eat."

Pampù surprises the students with a dish to share: cannellini beans cooked in fresh tomato sauce, with garlic, olive oil, salt and sage.

10 Pampù and the Pears

Pampù has bought a box of pears.

Dialogue between the pears:

"I'm happy I am not ripe yet, otherwise Pampù would separate me from you, and I would no longer be in your company."

"One pear under me must have gone bad, I have not heard from her since yesterday."

"Pampù has removed that one, so we do not get unhealthy too."

"I wonder what caused it to rot so fast."

"Pampù has added some apples to our box. I do not know why, but I was feeling better before this intrusion and I am very friendly."

"I think that the gas released by the apples speeds up our ripening process."

"Well, our destiny is to be eaten. Hopefully these apples will make us ripe at the same time so we will stay together till the end."

"Yes, this way we won't be taken out on separate days and none of us will have to be in this box alone."

11 Pampù and the Peaches

Pampù loves peaches. It is summer and her peach tree is full of peaches. She sees some on the ground but they are spoiled by worms. She picks some good ones from the tree, puts them in a basket and drives to her organic chemistry class.

Dialogue between the peaches:

"It is good to be together here in this basket, where no bird, squirrel, raccoon, insect or worm can bother us."

"Yes, at least till some alien put us on a plate!"

"Where are we? This is a strange place. I smell a peach fragrance that is not coming from us."

"Maybe these aliens not only like to grow and take care of us because we taste very good and we have a lot of nutrients but now they also try to reproduce our sweet fragrance."

"What would they do with our fragrance?"

"You know, the aliens are powerful manipulators of this universe and they go crazy for products that cost little and give them big gains, like making and selling perfumes. This seems to be the main game they like to play."

12 Pampù and the Poppies

It is June and the wheat field with beautiful golden ears is ready to be mowed and threshed. In the midst of the long wheat stems there are some short bright orange red heads sticking up and showing off an array of beautiful petals, the poppies. Poppies live well in that environment because they like the bright sunlight without being exposed to intense heat. They grow spontaneously, unlike the wheat that comes from the seeds planted in the ground by farmers. The wind blows the poppy seeds at different times, so some poppies reach maturity at the same time of the wheat, while others are still in buds. The machine to mow the wheat is about to enter the field. Pampù takes some pictures to capture the beauty of those colors before they are gone.

Dialogue between the poppies:

"The machine has arrived just in time. Like the wheat, I have dried seeds now. Later I can give life to many other poppies."

"Instead my flower buds are about to open up, the sepals will drop down but no one will be able to see my beautiful red petals. I will not be able to produce any seeds to continue my life cycle, no more spectacular blooming poppies from me."

"I am happy the wind brought me here at the perfect time. My seeds are enclosed in a nice capsule that will break open, they will drop and they will be together again on the ground. New plants will be born from them in the spring and the joy of our colors will continue on."

13 Pampù and the Flowers of the Linden Tree

It is June and Pampù is taking a walk in the park under the shade of a long row of a few hundred years old, tall linden trees. Her parents used to take her there with the stroller when she was little. She has always had the good memories of the strong, pleasant scent emanating from the flowers of those trees.

The flowers on the branches near Pampù notice how happy she looks when she breathes in their fragrance that is spread all over the air and they start wondering about their own role:

"Many aliens like to pick us from our branches and let us dry in the shade to make herbal teas. We are important, beautiful flowers."

"Well, not only the aliens like us, do you notice that during the day we are visited by bees?"

"Yes, why do bees like us too?"

"We have a sugary liquid that bees collect to make honey. Our honey tastes and smells so good that it stands out from all the other kinds of honey. And bees do not tear us apart to get our pollen!"

"Insects are attracted by our beauty and fragrance and when they land on us they help carry our pollen from one flower to another, thus facilitating insemination and reproduction so that we can become the fruit that contains the seeds".

"Then our survival depends on how good we look and smell!"

"Yes, and we are useful as fresh flowers, dried and to make honey! We liven up the life of the aliens with our fragrance, with delicious herbal teas and as a sweetener for their drinks!"

Pampù looks ecstatic. Her happy facial expression translates exactly what the flowers are saying.

14 Pampù and the Laurel

A laurel hedge is obstructing the view of the pool in the garden. Pampù loves that peaceful view, especially in summer when she likes to relax on the lounge chair after dinner to ease the stress of a busy day. Pampù looks close at the laurel to decide how much it should be trimmed and notices that another plant has been growing spontaneously in between. It is an eastern deciduous jasmine, but because it loses its leaves in winter it is more noticeable in summer when the leaves are back. Pampù sees that a laurel plant near that jasmine has fewer leaves than the rest and that it is losing its natural gloss, almost as it if was slowly dying.

Dialogue between the laurel plants:

"My friends, I'm kind to other plants, but my proximity to this jasmine that is becoming bigger and bigger is separating me from the rest of you. After I started losing my leaves, the birds, especially the robins, do not come any more to make their nests on my branches and the alien gardener keeps on trimming me hoping I could recover my strength this way, but it is not working and I feel increasingly excluded from your company."

"You're right, the hedge is no longer continuous and we miss you. Even Pampù seems sad when she looks at us. She loves us so much, I am sure she will find a solution."

Pampù is considering eradicating the intruder plant. She thinks that its roots may take away nutrients from the laurel and cause the laurel to die.

In autumn Pampù asks her gardener to remove the jasmine from the ground and transplant it by the fence on the other side of the property, to make sure it grows far from the laurel.

Next spring the sick laurel is not sick any more...

"What a happy time, I am strong again and my branches are full of new buds. I am still here, able to talk with you. After being sick and isolated for a while, now I feel alive, with my best friends."

15 Pampù and the Aloe Vera

Pampù asks a friend to take care of her plants for ten days while she visits her daughter out of town.

Soliloquy of an upset Aloe vera:

"I am the queen of the succulent plants, the Aloe Vera. I live in a sunny spot in my own pot next to some daisies. Pampù used to take good care of me and water me when I was thirsty. She loved my exotic look and she liked my sap on her skin when she got sunburnt. One week ago I almost drowned in too much water! I looked up and I saw a different alien. How could it be that she would give the daisies and me the same amount of water? Just because I live close to the daisies it does not mean that we are thirsty the same way. I store water, I am from the desert! I got scared but I hoped it would take her just a few days to get to know me better. Now I am worried, I am losing my usual development and I feel weaker and weaker. I may end dead without Pampù. Not all the aliens are alike then, just like us, succulent plants that we come in thousands of varieties. Pampù, where are you? Come back soon, before it is too late!"

16 Pampù and the Astroloba

Pampù empties a pot with some Astroloba plants.

Dialogue between the Astroloba:

"I'm happy of what is going on. Living together is beautiful but only if we have enough space. If we are too many, crowded side by side, our roots won't have enough of the nutrients from the soil that we need for our survival."

"I agree with you. But look, there are three new, large, empty pots over there. They might be for us!"

"I hope Pampù will take into account the close friendship we have developed and that she will put the ones of us that were in direct contact with each other in the same pot."

"Yes and the big plants will help the small ones during the transition, so they will feel protected."

"This division is necessary, it will take us a few days to adjust to the new environment and then we will be fine."

Pampù is very fast to arrange the Astroloba in the three pots with a lot of new potting soil.

"Now we have more space and with all this soil we will have plenty of nutrients!"

"We would have not been able to do all that by ourselves. Only the aliens are able to perform these miracles."

17 Pampù and the Camellia

Pampù has three camellia plants in a flower bed, two with white flowers and one in crimson. They are wonderful plants. With their attractive glossy-green foliage they add value and beauty to her garden in every season of the year, especially when they are in full bloom from winter to spring with their large flowers and rich petals.

Dialogue between the camellias:

"I'm happy to show all my flowers to Pampù because she always treats me with love, but not to the people passing by the fence. Some stranger has tried to reach my flowering branches, I do not like to be pulled and Pampù gets sad to see that."

"You are right, though I believe that Pampù cares for me more. She always stands by me longer. Do not be jealous, maybe she likes me better because my bright crimson flowers last longer than yours and my petals stay beautiful for more days. Your white flowers instead are immaculate only when the buds open up, but then it takes just a bit of extra water or wind to turn yellowish quickly."

"Unlike you, I make white flowers, however, I am luckier than you because my branches are the farthest from the fence and nobody can touch me."

Pampù decides to do something unusual to protect all her camellia from strangers. She sprinkles the flowering branches that are at easy reach through the fence with non-toxic glue so anybody trying to touch them would end up with their hands stuck and her camellia would be safe.

18 Pampù and the Euphorbia

Pampù has some Euphorbia plants that did not look healthy last winter, although she had put them in a spot that looked ideal, on a sunny window sill. They had lost their leaves and only in the spring they started recovering their vegetative growth, filling up with leaves and small flowers of an intense pink color. This year at the beginning of winter Pampù decides to move the Euphorbias outside. She puts them in a corner of the patio where the fence would protect them from cold air drafts and where they would be more exposed to the sun than if she kept them inside.

Dialogue between the Euphorbias:

°I do not know this location, but I like it."

"Maybe another alien, not Pampù, put us here."

"I do not think so because when I was lifted at the beginning of the cold season to be moved from the window sill to here I felt the touch of Pampù' s gentle hands."

"Then our alien is the same but she must have had a change of heart."

"What do you think happened to her?"

"She may feel happier this year and so she takes better care of us."

"Maybe, but Pampù has always loved us. I believe that when she saw us in such a poor shape last winter, without any leaves, she must have felt bad, not for how ugly we looked but because she realized we were not doing well where we were. So she has moved us to help us stay healthy this winter."

"Now that you say that I understand why Pampù used to spread on us a thin white membrane every day early mornings when it was cold and then she would remove it around noon when there was some warm sunshine. She was trying to protect us from the cold".

"Or she may nanny us selfishly hoping to enjoy the beauty of our flowers without any down time. Actually, this is a mean thought because now that she has put us outside by the wall she could not see our flowers since she is always inside the house in winter."

"Yes, we are really fortunate to be with an alien who is so caring. Pampù moves us under the sun in summer and to this sheltered spot in winter to help us live well together all year round."

Pampù is so happy to have found the perfect winter location for her Euphorbia that she does not even care that the patio looks too crowded in that corner.

19 Pampù and the Ferns

Pampù notices that some ferns that had spontaneously grown in a large pot, home of an acanthus plant, have become bigger. They are taking too much space, almost suffocating the acanthus. Should she pull them out and throw them in the trash where they would find a sure death or should she save them? Pampù loves plants so she has to find another place for them, but where? She already has a lot of ferns. Who could she give them to? Who does she know that loves plants too? Hey, her friend Biba! Pampù buys a nice pot for the ferns and she takes them to Biba.

Dialogue between the ferns:

"I wonder why Pampù has removed us from the pot where we had lived for more than two years."

"She has favored the acanthus plant, though it seems to me that we are more decorative."

"Pampù may like the acanthus more because the acanthus leaves are very famous. The Greeks loved to use acanthus leaves as ornamental elements in their architectural wonders. There are columns with Corinthian capitals decorated with acanthus leaves in many churches."

"We may not be famous, but we are lucky because now we are in a bigger and more beautiful pot, all for us. We are still together and we have a lot of room to grow and to expand our family. We should not be angry at Pampù."

Pampù always checks on the ferns when she visits her friend Biba. She is happy they are doing great.

20 Pampù and the Oaks

Pampù has a long row of oak trees on one side of her fence. They must have lived there over a hundred years because they have big trunks. They are the kind of oaks that loses leaves in winter. Although in winter time they are not beautiful, they are useful because without leaves they allow more natural light in her house. They were healthy and they used to produce so many acorns in the season of the harvest that the peasants in the neighborhood liked to collect them up as food for their pigs. But things are about to change when the country lane by her property becomes a busy road, with traffic day and night. All her oak trees start getting sick.

Dialogue between the oaks:

"I have not been feeling good recently. There is something extra in the air that bothers me. When there was no traffic I was breathing healthy oxygen, now with all these cars I smell some kind of bad gas."

"It is the exhaust gas from cars. The aliens call it carbon dioxide. It is toxic and they force it on us all day long"

"Then why do some aliens tell their students that plants breathe only at night?"

"Maybe some aliens get it wrong because they think of us simply as oxygen producers. Our green parts function as a lab to produce oxygen only when there is light, during daytime. With this activity we keep everybody alive. Nobody could survive without oxygen in the air. But besides producing oxygen at daytime, we always breathe, day and night, just like the aliens and the animals."

"We have to continue producing oxygen for us and for everybody else. Let's hope that those aliens who devote their lives studying pollution can fuel their cars with something that won't be harmful to any living being."

Pampù decides to go around her neighborhood asking to sign a petition to restrict traffic to local residents. With fewer cars the air would be cleaner and the oaks would be healthier.

ABOUT THE AUTHOR

Laura Ebrahimi is originally from Tuscany, in Italy. After College she visited many countries, then she moved to the United States, first exploring San Francisco and Los Angeles, later on settling down in the Seattle area, where she has raised her two children, Characterized by an eclectic personality, her interests embrace many fields. In these tales she gives plants a voice, while being entertaining and educational.